DON'T THINK & GROW RICH

SURESH MANSHARAMANI

PRABHAT
PAPERBACKS

Published by

PRABHAT PAPERBACKS

An Imprint of Prabhat Prakashan Pvt. Ltd.
4/19 Asaf Ali Road,
New Delhi–110 002 (INDIA)
e-mail: prabhatbooks@gmail.com

ISBN 978-93-5521-131-6

DON'T THINK & GROW RICH

by Suresh Mansharamani

Edition
2022

Price
₹ 195 (Rupees One Hundred Ninety Five Only)

Printed at
Sanjay Printer, Sahibabad

Dedicated to that Most Capricious
Never-to-be-Understood Weather Rocky
Provokingly Incorruptible and Absolutely
Necessary Person,
THE GENTLE READER

Author's Note

The book, Don't Think and Grow Rich has some fundamental principles on how individuals make decisions. It will help you comprehend why humans make mistakes in making judgments and how to spot warning indications that you will make one.

Reading this book could have had a profound impact on your worldview. The chapters have been supported by the scientific research and studies conducted globally. Each chapter carries the author's first-hand life learnings to make them more relatable. Real-life instances can make readers closer to the concepts being discussed in the book.

Don't Think and Grow Rich provides a new perspective on behaviors and judgments.

The reader can apply some of the knowledge to situations where they see people themselves relying too much on thinking. The important thing is to recognize whether we are just giving thoughts to our decisions or becoming victims of the Paralysis of Analysis.

This book on making once-in-a-lifetime decisions provides valuable tips on how to improve your ability to make quick-thinking, intuitive judgments. But what about more critical decisions, the ones that will affect our lives for years, if not centuries? The most powerful stories of the author's life revolve around these kinds of decisions:

- where to live
- what to believe
- whether to start a company or business
- how to shut down his business

This book draws principles from cognitive science, social psychology, military strategy, and great works of literature, and it is full of wonderfully written narratives and innovative discoveries. Everyone believes that we live in a time when people have short attention spans, yet we've learned a lot about making long-term judgments over the past several decades. Mr. Suresh Mansharamani presents a convincing argument for more creative and deliberate decision-making. He contends that we make better decisions when we break free from the myopia of single-scale thinking and create ways for considering all relevant elements. There is no one-size-fits-all strategy for making critical decisions that may change the trajectory of a person, an organization, or a civilization. However, Don't Think and Grow Rich illustrates how we might approach these decisions more effectively and understand the subtle wisdom of choices that built our more significant social history.

❑

Acknowledgements

I'd like to take this opportunity to thank the Universe as well as everyone who has had an impact on my life. This book is the final outcome of more than four decades of experience, learning, practicing, and researching. I had the good fortune to learn from trainers such as Blair Singer, Gulraj Shahpuri, and T. Harv Eker. I am grateful to each of them for the wisdom they have shared as well as the influence they have had in my life.

Gulraj Shahpuri, a dear friend who taught me the ABCs of public speaking, gave me my first public speaking experience. Blair Singer provided me with a Train the Trainer Certification. I enrolled in a number of

T. Harv Eker Academy online courses. I am eternally grateful to each and every one of my coaches.

I'd like to thank all of my friends, colleagues, Tajurba members, and leadership teams for giving me the opportunity to discuss my ideas with them. The debates and discussions I had with them were extremely beneficial in terms of structuring this book. I interviewed a number of Tajurba members. They all shared their perspectives with me, which aided in the development of this book. I owe them a great debt of gratitude.

I am grateful to Ms. Avinasha Sharma for her editing help, astute analysis, and ongoing assistance in bringing my experiences to life.

Last but not least, I want to thank my wife Uma, my sons Rahul and Tarun, and my daughter-in-law Deeksha for always being there for me and encouraging me.

❑

Contents

CHAPTER 1

How 'Don't Think....' Differs From the Legendary One

D*on't Think and Grow Rich* is neither a replica of the masterpiece by Napoleon Hill's masterwork, nor is it a book in opposition to the one written by the famed author who was on a mission to spread his philosophy of leadership, self-motivation, and individual accomplishment. Think and Grow Rich is a monument to personal success and the cornerstone of modern motivation.

So, what else does this book have to offer? I'd want to go right to the point of this book's existence and purpose.

Don't Think and Grow Rich is a supplement to Napoleon's material. His beliefs are shown by the stories of Andrew Carnegie, Thomas Edison, Henry Ford, and other millionaires of Napoleon's time. This book will unfold the secrets to making money by making quick decisions in life. It will demonstrate not just what to do but also how to accomplish it. You will have learned the secret of genuine and enduring success after studying and using the simple, fundamental strategies given here.

Money and material things are necessary for physical and mental freedom. However, some may say that the most valuable of all wealth can only be assessed in terms of long-term friendships, loving family relationships, understanding between business associates, and introspective harmony that brings true peace of mind! Everyone who reads, comprehends, and applies this philosophy will better attract and experience these spiritual values.

The main aim is to help you avoid overthinking or negative thinking when you make rapid and informed judgments without being paralyzed by analysis. This aids in the development of solid commercial connections, the completion of sales more quickly, and the accumulation of wealth.

GET READY! When you are exposed to the effect of this philosophy, you may have a changed life, which may help you navigate your path through life with harmony and understanding and prepare you for the acquisition of enormous financial wealth.

Let me list some of the advantages I've gained in my life as a result of making swift decisions:

Quick decision-making is your competitive advantage

Today, making rapid judgments is possibly the most important for a business.

Why is speed so important? Because it is the thing that allows you to stay ahead of your competitors in a fast-paced environment.

Much research has been conducted that demonstrates a clear relationship between decision effectiveness and corporate performance.

It discovered that high-performing organizations made faster, less effort, and more frequently than their low-performing counterparts. Companies that mulled over decisions for months, on the other hand, saw their development stall as their competitors overtook them.

Making quick decisions saves time and money.

Whether you believe your company is excellent or awful at making decisions, the fact is that most businesses can enhance their decision-making efficacy.

In my over four decades of experience in many types of enterprises, I have met hundreds of people and discovered that just 20% of them felt their organizations excelled in decision-making. Furthermore, most respondents claimed that most of their time spent on decision-making is wasted. This was true for little, regular decisions and significant, life-changing decisions.

People who felt their company excelled at decision-making were twice as likely to report excellent returns on their most recent decisions, demonstrating that sluggish decision-making costs organizations both time and money.

The researchers also discovered something interesting: "Faster judgments tend to be higher quality, implying that speed does not undermine the validity of a particular decision. Suitable decision-making methods, on the other hand, tend to produce decisions that are both high-quality and timely."

Employees who participate in decision-making are more likely to be engaged.

Slow decision-making has an impact not just on income but also on staff engagement. The Institute for Employment Studies examined data from over 10,000 employees to determine the characteristics that have the most significant effect on employee engagement.

They discovered that the most powerful driver of all is a sense of being respected and involved, with participation in decision-making being crucial to this. Employees who are not given the authority to make decisions and rely on leadership for guidance rapidly get disenchanted.

They become less committed to the firm, and as a result, their performance declines. They may even start looking for alternative opportunities. Workers can assist in moving the firm ahead if decision-making is delegated, and employees may play an active part. This contributes to their enthusiasm for both their work and their employer.

Trust is required for quick decision-making

Delegating choices and enabling staff to get things done implies that issues are handled faster, and opportunities are capitalized on instead of being squandered due to indecision. It also allows senior executives to focus on the more significant concerns, while employees on the front lines can make the best decisions for their departments.

Cloverpop CEO Erik Larson writes for Forbes that the best-performing organizations display trust: "Successful businesses lean into the need for trust by concentrating on delegation, openness, and accountability."

These organizations create a "triangle of trust" through delegation, openness, and accountability, which allows them to make faster and better decisions. "They engage their people, innovate and adapt, and execute swiftly and efficiently," Larson explains.

Rapid decision-making is being de-risked

While quick decisions are beneficial for corporations, hasty decisions are not. So, how can you expedite things while avoiding mistakes? Experience and skill are practical, yet even experienced individuals might make the wrong decision.

The Nobel Prize recipient for his work on cognitive biases that influence human decision-making, psychologist Daniel Kahneman, observes: "Intuition feels the same when it's incorrect and when it's right, and that's the issue."

However, judgments do not have to be based only on intuition; incorporating facts may significantly boost confidence in your conclusions.

Data-driven conclusions are more accessible for everyone to accept since data eliminate prejudice and subjectivity. The numbers point you in the right direction.

Of course, data collection might take time, but some data sources are both rapid and dependable. With Attest, you can quickly reach out to thousands of people to gather the information you want. You may instantly reach out to thousands of individuals using Attest to obtain the information you need. With Attest, you can rapidly reach out to thousands of people to gather the information you need to make quick, fact-based choices.

Here are a few instances of how Attest clients have lately utilized the platform to inform their decisions:

A supermarket wanted to see what customers thought of its proposed new café menu, and the results were quite positive.

A flower delivery firm wanted to debut in France and Germany but realized it would need to adjust a key component of its offering first.

During COVID-19, a fitness company pondered if it needed to pivot and learned that users desired online tools.

An insurance firm explored altering its name, but market research in five areas revealed that the new name was unpopular.

Increase the speed with which you make judgments, and you will outperform your competitors

Slow decision-making is a significant reason why businesses fall behind. It stymies go-to-market strategies and inhibits innovative ideas from being implemented on time. There are several examples of what occurs when corporations postpone the delivery.

Consider Blockbuster Video, which could not compete with online streaming services due to its unwillingness to embrace the internet. Then there's BlackBerry, which suffered due to underestimating Apple and failing to adapt to the market.

To win, you must always be one step ahead of the competition. And to do so, your company must be agile — constructed like a speedboat rather than a massive ship that takes forever to alter course.

The destruction of bureaucratic structures is key to this. To accomplish this, one needs to delegate decision-making and provide people with the information they require to influence their decisions. What used to happen in months or years is now completed in hours. And what about your competitors? They've been left in a cloud of dust!

Learning From My Experiences

'Experience speaks for itself in a voice, which is deep and rich to the visionary and inaudible to the ignorant.'

My journey of being an entrepreneur and business coach started way back in the 1980s, when opportunities didn't knock the doors frequently. Money requirements were high in my family, and I was on the lookout for a chance to gain the most of it. I inherited being industrious from my parents, who have been quite supportive in most of my decisions. But I followed my instincts religiously when it came to making decisions for my life.

I commenced my career as a job seeker to earn a respectable living. Getting a four-figure salary was my dream in those days when I stepped into my 20s. My first job was to sell a washing soap named 'Booby,' and I was paid INR 300. I seized the chance with both hands, believing that anything huge begins with small measures. So, unlike my friends and relatives, I didn't wait for something great to happen in my life; instead, I took a quick decision to give my career a start. My second job was with a Garment exporter, which laid the foundations of business skills in my life. Although my salary was quite the same, I preferred experience to monetary gain and started expanding my learning horizons.

I started working for more than I was getting. This was the phase in my life wherein I realized that I needed to be more than ordinary to become rich. I kept my eyes and ears alert in the company of experienced individuals to give my vision a profound form. There was a resounding call within me to put my hard work into whatever little I was getting to shape my life. My job was to maintain the company's accounts, but I started learning the production and purchase department basics. I worked for long hours, which had increased my boss's dependency on me. I got a promotion as the Manager with a 50% raise in my salary.

Another quick decision I took during those days was not to ask for overtime benefits as I realized that Managers never ask for overtime; instead, their work confers the benefits on them.

I never thought that the opportunities that seemed to be relatively small could be a game-changer in my life. My credibility started speaking for me, and other garment exporters wished to employ me due to my result-oriented approach towards my work. I was offered three times more than the salary I was getting that time, along with a new bike. This was quite emphatic as it was the first bike in my family during the '80s.

These quick decisions increased my confidence and formulated the skills required to undertake risks in my life.

❑

CHAPTER 2

Cognitive Skills for Good Decision-making

The most significant findings have verified what many people have long suspected: human thinking and judgment are not always rational in the last five decades. By this, I mean that in a scenario when someone needs to make a choice, she will frequently choose a conclusion that "leaps" to her rather than one that combines the structure of the problem, facts accessible instantly, and data that should be obtained. Intuition and logic lead to the same conclusion; thus, it isn't a problem. However, intuition often leads to poor judgment in retrospect to state the obvious. How many times have you wondered, "Why didn't I think of it sooner?"

This flaw in our decision-making arises from the fact that our intuition may be "hacked" by others to cause us to act in ways that are not in our best interests. In the actual world, motivated framing and packaging of information occur all the time. There's something for everyone, from Tinder to LinkedIn profiles to what's written on yogurt. What isn't expressed is frequently more essential than what is. For example, if there were two yogurt brands on the shelf, one said "80 percent fat-free" and the other said "20 percent fat added," Which one would you choose? Do you consider the second and third-order ramifications of discounts on your company's image when a sales manager recommends a deal to increase turnover towards the end of the month?

What if the sales manager had stated, "Giving discounts will harm our reputation as a firm that is confident in its products, but we will surely boost income." "Are we alright with that?"

The letters "B" and "13" have the same shape. Others can "hack" your judgments by presenting them to you in specific packaging.

Such framing effects are pretty widespread in everyday life and business. The problem isn't that intuition is flawed. It is instrumental in ordinary circumstances. You wouldn't want to "reason" which ice cream to eat when the stakes are low. My issue is that we only learn about the stakes after the fact. Oh-shit moments occur when we apply our intuition on seemingly minor issues that turn out to be significant.

This is a risky scenario. A rider believes that not wearing a helmet is acceptable because it's a short journey to work.

My intuition improves with each error, although I would avoid making such blunders. What if a second-order impact threatens the company's existence? For example, I once made the little choice to remove sugary drinks (Coke and Pepsi) from the corporate canteen. People, to my surprise, mistook it for a cost-cutting move rather than a health-related purpose. I felt I was making a straightforward decision for the team's sake. But I never thought that the same attitude could be interpreted differently.

Now I understand that "experience" in business is the accumulation of blunders that a person has utilized to broaden their "circle of available knowledge." Reflecting on mistakes allows what comes to mind to be easily expanded, allowing experienced people to make better decisions. You will make the same mistakes if you do not reflect. Each error is an opportunity to train intuition.

Keeping cognitive biases at bay

When discussing cognitive biases, the author of the best-selling book Thinking Fast and Slow, Daniel Kahneman, is the first one that comes to mind. I want to share a few pointers on avoiding cognitive biases:

1. Avoid making judgments under time constraints.

When we decide under duress, our capacity to notice and fix a mistake in judgment suffers dramatically. It is only rare when it is not possible to take extra time to choose. Even in a car collision, it is prudent to pause for a moment before reacting. At work, this time constraint on decision-making is frequently self-imposed. Vague comments like "we need to choose the conclusion of this 30-minute discussion" or "speed is all that matters" actively work against sound decision-making. I know these phrases are meaningless because I used them until I started thinking about it and wondering why a meeting should finish with a choice when none is apparent. There is no wisdom in making a hasty judgment that turns out to be incorrect.

Jeff Bezos gave the following advice in his 2016 shareholder letter:

Some judgments are crucial and irreversible or almost so — one-way doors – and must be made systematically, carefully, slowly, and with much consideration and consultation. You can't come back to where you were if you step through and don't like what you see on the other side. These are referred to as Type 1 decisions. Most decisions, however, are adjustable and reversible — they are two-way doors. You don't have to live with the effects of a poor Type 2 decision for that long. You can go back through if you reopen the door. Type 2 judgments may and should be made swiftly by people with excellent reviews or small groups.

This, of course, works for him. Over the previous 20+ years of operating Amazon, he has incorporated tens of hundreds of mental models into his intuition. So what comes to mind instinctively for him will be considerably different from (and indeed a superset of) what comes to mind for you.

Because the implications of your actions are unknown ahead of time at work, a valuable "trick" to recognize when not to take decisions under a time constraint is when you are in a job that affects many other humans. The actions of a CEO have a rippling influence on staff, customers, and shareholders. The actions of a software engineer have an impact on all clients (seemingly innocent changes usually introduce security loopholes). On the other hand, a salesperson can only cause harm.

2. Do not make decisions when intellectually engaged in another task.

According to research, when participants must hold some numbers in their heads while completing a puzzle, their performance suffers. This problem is exacerbated at work since those with the most potential to create harm through a false choice (CEOs, VPs, and senior managers) are generally the ones who are dragged into most meetings. You know how mentally draining they can be when you have been at an appointment with a personal agenda (rather than being there because your boss asked you to). Inevitably, the hangover of an unsolved problem from one meeting follows you to the next, and you perform poorly in both.

Cognitive capacity becomes the limiting element for value generation for everyone who makes a career by applying brains to issues. It doesn't matter how many emails you respond to or how many lines of code you produce. What counts is the quality of your thought and decision-making.

At work, I utilize a workaround in which I set out time on the calendar for myself to think. During that period, I don't check emails or attend meetings. Paul Graham refers to this as maker hours, and it has worked brilliantly for me (I was inspired to use this strategy by Cal Newport's Deep Work). In addition, I make a deliberate effort to attend only one critical meeting every day. I do not particularly appreciate having a full calendar because I know I won't contribute the value required after the first meeting.

3. If you are a "morning person," don't make decisions in the evening (and vice versa)

At various periods of the day, different people feel more energized. Some people are night owls, but I'm a night person who knows I can't work well in the morning. Determine when you are most productive and set aside that time for yourself. This is why my maker's hours are from 10:30 am to 2 am, and I avoid working early mornings.

4. Be cautious if you are pleased with a decision.

This may seem counter-intuitive, yet a study shows that happy individuals make poor judgments. The explanation for this is that joyful individuals cannot recognize flaws in their intuition (and because they cannot detect such errors, their cognition cannot remedy such mistakes). This fallacy arises just because we avoid sadness, and in choices when the outcome is crucial to us, we grasp on to any good evidence that jumps out at us (while the negative data is ignored). Entrepreneurs must be cautious because they are so determined to succeed that they overestimate the facts in their favor. If you send an email to 100 individuals and one answers positively, your attention is drawn to the positive things the respondent says rather than the fact that 99 others did not respond. The lack of data is a data point to be interpreted.

Being skeptical about obvious decisions allows us to look for ways things may go wrong (how it will succeed comes with a stake in the judgment). It's an exceedingly tough hack to implement since this way of thinking attacks our ego. What works for me is to write down everything about a decision that makes me happy and then intentionally drive myself to write out all the reasons why the same thing may fail and make me upset. (Because I start reasoning why failures wouldn't happen if I think about it, I had to write.) After I've written down the benefits and disadvantages, I don't act right away but instead wait to be cognitively occupied with something else. When I return, I view the same list with new eyes and analyze it more objectively than before (like a non-interested party).

This hack is also applicable to fresh concepts that I come across. When I become enthusiastic about an issue, I Google" versus "or "critique," and Google autocomplete with opposing viewpoints that my enthused self would not have discovered. (For instance, see "blockchain critique" or "universal basic income criticism").

Keep an eye on your happiness, especially if you are anxious for something to succeed. Who said it was simple to think better?

5. Create a statistical mindset in oneself.

Statistical reasoning is complex; therefore, it does not come to us naturally. Humans overestimate low and high probability while ignoring meager and highly high possibilities. Even physicians are susceptible to non-statistical reasoning. Consider the following scenario: (that can very well happen in the real world).

Breast cancer affects around 1% of women aged 40-50. Eighty percent of mammograms detect it (20 percent miss it). Breast cancer is detected in 9.6 percent of mammograms when it is not present (and therefore, 90.4 percent correctly return a negative result).

You get mammography, and the results are positive. What is the likelihood that you have cancer?

Before you continue reading, express your gut instinct. Thought? Relax for a moment and consider your options before making a decision. What's your response now?

The average response rate for physicians in charge of guiding patients is close to 75%. What is your response? (In this situation, the true answer to how likely you are to get cancer if the test is positive is less than 10%.) Surprised?

I encourage becoming acquainted with the Bayes way of thinking since it can help you make better judgments in several situations:

If a product's sales are expanding, should you recruit more salespeople? (Knowledge of fluctuations and the distinction between correlation and causation is helpful here.)

The average customer satisfaction score was 80 percent. Is that reason to rejoice? (Knowing that averages remove information about the distribution helps here.)

90% of people that start a business fail within the first 2-3 years.

Should you take the chance? (Here, adopting 90% as a Bayesian prior but then including knowledge regarding failure reasons and selecting which things work for you and which work against you helps.)

Learning From My Experiences

'Knowledge comes from learning,
Experience comes from living.
A life without problems,
Is just like a school without lessons.'

Life is not all about all the good decisions and risks we undertake. I also learned from the decisions that didn't prove favorable for me. My Garment export business was going quite well, but the wrong decision to run it on autopilot proved disastrous for my family and me. I wished solid technical advancements and systems would have supported us in those days due to a lack of technical support. We decided to open offices in Frankfurt and New York, but we ended up losing much money as it was challenging to meet the expenses and salary of the employees.

We could not bear the losses and decided to shut down our 25 years of Garment Export business.

The decision to shut down a legacy that was nurtured with years of hard work was a wrong decision on my part. If only I could have sought help from a coach or mentor, it could have been the other way round, but such support was rarely available those days. I also realized that my overconfidence in achieving success in every decision I took in my life was also one of the reasons for my wrong decision. As mature business owners, we must also weigh our risks before making a quick decision. We must keep pros and cons in mind before initiating a profound step as hasty choices prove to be highly disastrous.

The loss of the Garment Export Business took away another decade of my life as I tried my hand at several small businesses but could not succeed. Times were tough as survival of the means was in question. But determination and never giving up spirit kept me going. Although today when I look back, I realize that my decisions were not very thoughtful during those days. Therefore, they resulted in a loss of time and money.

It was 2006, and following the footsteps of Netflix's success in the US, we tried to implement an e-commerce business of online DVD rental in India. We didn't analyze that piracy is rampant in India, and people would not be interested in watching original movies after the two months of theatre release. Moreover, pirated copies were available on the same day. Again, a couple of crores went in the drain in our Moviemart. in business.

At the same time, a few other businesses such as Retail shops and Real Estate also didn't work for us. I started enhancing my knowledge and joined a weekend college to learn financial planning. It was almost the end of 2006 when my financial condition started improving with wealth management and insurance advisory services, but still, a lot more was required to cover up my losses.

What I learned over these years was that we need to understand the difference between overthinking and not thinking at all. We should not overthink letting the opportunity go, but at the same time, making wrong decisions without pondering may let you feel regret over your choices.

'Mistakes are painful, but collections of mistakes are an experience years later.'

❑

CHAPTER 3

The Role of Attention in Decision-making Process

According to a traditional decision-making perspective, attention first serves to obtain the most relevant and necessary information for choosing between options. As a result, the role of attention is essentially passive. However, an alternate viewpoint that has gained support in recent years, particularly with the help of eye-tracking studies, contends that attention plays a more active role in choice processes, impacting decision formation.

This is a crucial lesson Orquin and Mueller Loose conveyed in their analysis of the function of attention in decision-making, as evidenced by eye-movement tracking and subsequent fixations. The researchers' method, on the other hand, is unusual: They do not limit themselves to the area of decision-making; instead, they begin their assessment and analysis of data with theories or models of tasks similar to or connected to decision-making (e.g., perception, information processing, visual search, working memory, top-down and bottom-up processes, problem-solving). Then they attempt to project how the attention functions in such activities may project to or be manifested in decision processes.

Learning From My Experiences Furthermore, Orquin and Mueller Loose investigate the extent to which the evidence corresponds with four different hypotheses and accompanying decision-making models (i.e., whether empirical evidence substantiates or refutes assumptions or conclusions in each theory).

Based on eye-tracking in decision-making research, they assess data from a prior study on similar or related activities that might also be tracked, particularly in choice tasks, and evaluate this evidence in the light of the different decision-making theories.

1. Rational models;

2. Bounded rationality models;

3. Evidence accumulation models

The rational and restricted rationality models argue more forcefully that the role of attention is to capture the information needed to make a choice.' Strong analytical models maintain that all relevant, accessible information regarding option alternatives would be attended to and considered, whereas relaxed, rational models allow for the potential of part of the information not being listened to (e.g., attributes or object [product] features).

According to bounded rationality models, information is obtained only as needed by the decision rules. The two other models are more adaptable in terms of how information is gathered and used and its impact on the decision-making process and outcome. However, it is claimed that all four theories are deficient in examining the role and function of attention in choice processes, to varying degrees, with at least some of their assumptions being rejected by the data assessed.

Selected observations from Orquin and Mueller Loose's review are cited here only briefly to shed emphasis on the importance of attention in consumer decision-making.

A critical question in decision-making is how information enters the decision process and chooses. This data may be obtained by attention led by a top-down (goal-driven) process, or it can be collected by a bottom-up (stimulus-based) attentional approach. The intertwining of two methods while choosing is critical in this sector, with several ramifications. A more exceptional task experience and increased visualization comprehension expertise may drive a more efficient selection process.

The combination of bottom-up and top-down processing can increase attention capture and improve the visual acuity of observed objects. The saliency of a visual stimulus impacts the bottom-up attention. Still, it may not take effect when task demands on attention are intense, and top-down commands for attention are prioritized. According to decision-making studies, aesthetically appealing alternatives or features are more likely to catch attention and influence the choice in their favor.

Working memory and 'immediate' attention interact in the following way: As a load of information fixated grows, more components are transmitted to working memory, and information is retrieved from there for processing; however, as the strain on working memory grows, consumers resort to re-fixating information pieces and considering them instantaneously or just-in-time (i.e., fixations are thus used as external memory space). This form of interaction has been observed in problem-solving activities. For example, the trade-off between working memory and fixations or re-fixations in choice tasks can be seen in alternative comparisons. Higher information complexity and choice difficulty (owing to more remarkable similarity between options) may need more effort (operations) in collecting and processing information. However, learning can expedite the process.

Processing of visual objects is another area with intriguing implications: previous research has demonstrated that visible items are not recorded as complete representations (e.g., realistic product graphics), and feature binding is very selective. As a result, encoding specific features during an object-stimulus fixation may be goal-driven. Re-fixation can refer to particular object [product] features as needed in a choice task, saving on working memory capacity.

Consumers tend to acquire a bias toward a preferred choice during a decision-making activity. This option would receive more fixations. There is a more significant chance of picking the last fixated alternative. A desired or preferred characteristic might benefit from a similar impact by receiving more frequent attention (i.e., fixations). However, the authors highlight a challenge in proving evidence accumulation models: whether the increased possibility of a more focused option being picked is due to its higher utility or more significant exposure. They propose a soft model version to provide a more substantial influence of prolonged mere exposure, leading to selecting an alternative. They say that a downstream effect of attention from perception to decision via a bottom-up process may act as a gatekeeper for other options entering a consideration set. It is emphasized that a downstream impact resulting from a bottom-up approach is distinct from a utility effect since the former is stimulus-driven while the latter is goal-driven.

Following constrained rationality theory, heuristics shape attention patterns driven by the information that a heuristic requires (e.g., by alternative or by attribute). However, eye-tracking experiments to follow the course of decision processes could not confirm the patterns of heuristics utilized as stated in the literature. More formally, investigations failed to prove the idea that heuristics in use may be deduced from attention patterns. Inferences are more difficult to make when consumers switch between alternative-wise and attribute-wise criteria during a choice job. The information cues encountered during the decision process can change the course of the decision strategy.

In summary, Orquin and Mueller Loose reach the following conclusions about decision-making theories:

1. More robust support for the relaxed, rational model over the firm model is required.

2. There is a two-way relationship between decision rules and attention. Both top-down and bottom-up processes drive engagement.

The chosen alternative is more likely to experience fixations during the choice task, while the final option is fixated.

Following the evaluation, I'd want to make a few closing remarks:

Orquin and Mueller Loose provide an essential and intriguing viewpoint on the function of [visual] attention in decision-making and choice by projecting it from similar or related activities. Furthermore, relevance is improved because associated activities are integrated into decision-making tasks. In terms of attracting attention, this appeal is consistent with the authors' findings. Furthermore, such research must consider real-world events and locations where customers judge.

Consider the research by Chandon, Hutchinson, Bradlow, and Young (2009) on the trade-off between visual lift (stimulus-based) and brand equity (memory-based) in retail establishments; this study integrated eye-tracking with scanner purchase data. However, it is worth investigating an alternate video tracking technique utilized by Hui, Huang, Suher, and Inman (2013) to study the relationships between planned and unplanned considerations and actual purchases (video tracking was applied in parallel with path tracking).

Refer to Glaholt and Reingold (2011) for a review and experiment with eye-tracking (choice bias), but consider the more critical viewpoint offered by Reisen, Hoffrage, and Mast (2008) after they evaluated several approaches of interactive process tracing. Reisen and his colleagues were less confident that measuring eye movements outperformed recording mouse movements to detect decision strategies when customers gathered information.

A significant portion of the research in this subject use eye-tracking measurement with concentrated presentations of information on alternatives and their features. Although information matrices (or boards) are the most common and known format, we may also find various visual formats such as networks, trees, stacked wheels, and more art-creative diagram drawings. Physical shop shelf displays have full displays and online and mobile app screen displays.

However, on many instances of choice tasks (e.g., durables, more costly items), consumers gather information across numerous sessions while making their selections. That is, the decision-making process takes time. Consumers may save certain information pieces or signals for subsequent processing and integration during each session, or they may carry out an intermediate stage in their chosen approach. Consumers may use aids such as paper notes and computer spreadsheets if the information is finally integrated, but they are not required to do so.

Orquin and Mueller Loose allude to eye-tracking effects deriving from spatial dispersion of information elements in a visual display (i.e., distance length of saccades). These studies do not consider the temporal distribution of information. However, cell phones nowadays can help close the gap by allowing customers to gain knowledge in-store while accessing further information from other sources on their smartphones.

Finally, while eye-tracking can give evidence regarding attention to stimuli and information signals, it cannot directly tell researchers about other dimensions such as information meaning and valence. Measures such as the frequency and duration of fixations can imply the importance of data to consumers. However, other methods are required to reveal additional dimensions, particularly from the conscious perspective of consumers.

The review of Orquin and Mueller Loose reveals the numerous ways attention can function during decision tasks, including top-down and bottom-up processes working in tandem, toggling between fixations and memory, a two-way relationship between decision strategies and visual attention, choice bias, and more. But, most importantly, we can learn about the dynamics of the function of concentration in consumer decision-making from this review.

Learning From My Experiences

"Whenever you see a successful business, someone once made a courageous decision."

– Peter F. Drucker

Grabbing the attention of your seniors and fulfilling the targets with a stimulus before has been quite a prominent way to make effective decisions in life. There were many instances in my life which motivated me to work hard to grab the attention of my boss or clients. I want to quote an amusing example.

One of my Marwadi boss called me in the garment factory and said that if I could complete the order of 50000 units in a month, which was double what the factory was producing those days, he would buy a Raymond suit for me. One can relate this incident to his life as most of us face similar challenging situations. We are often expected to fulfill the targets set before us. I also decided not to go home for a month and worked till late at night. But when you are at a managerial level, you need to transfer your zeal to your workers. Here, my role as a motivator played a vital role as I inspired my team to work as hard as I wished to work.

Our collective efforts bore fruits in a fortnight, and the order was completed in stipulated time.

It was not only the Raymond suit that gratified me, but the happiness of hitting the targets before the deadline made me thrilled.

This was when I realized that paying attention to the opportunities and taking quick actions with all my dedicated efforts to avail them can pave the way to success in my life. Therefore, I started putting all my efforts into exploring opportunities and gaining the best out of them. Later in this book, I would be quoting a couple of more instances wherein quick decisions with paralysis of the analysis proved a boon to my journey.

❑

CHAPTER 4

The Science of Rational Snap/Quick Decision-making

You've spent many hours preparing for the job interview. You've done your best to anticipate every question your potential new employers may throw at you. You pay careful consideration to every aspect, such as remembering to sit up straight, look them in the eyes, deliver a solid handshake, and tell them what they want to hear.

Regardless of how hard you work to create a good impression, the interview will end when the recruiters see you.

We've already chosen whether we want to hire, date, despise, or make friends with someone we're meeting for the first time before we've even finished blinking. Our first impressions color our interactions with other individuals. According to the study, all of this occurs outside of our consciousness, in the unconscious processes of the mind.

As the adage goes, "judge a book by its cover" has been the subject of much psychological research. The science of snap judgments entails more than simply determining what we can tell each other by glancing at each other. Knowing how individuals judge one other daily has important implications for detecting and reducing implicit bias, discrimination, and stereotyping.

We go through a sophisticated and complex process of detecting indicators that reveal other people's characteristics. Then, whether we're choosing a clerk at the grocery store or participants for a local ball game, we perform a series of computations in our heads to forecast how they'll respond.

Even when we have much knowledge, a hasty judgment takes precedence over decision-making. Billions of dollars are spent worldwide to advance political campaigns. The platform, voting record, experience, and credentials of a candidate are all scrutinized by voters and the media. However, studies have shown that we are influenced by the candidate's looks when we enter the voting booth. In a 2005 research, students at Princeton University were given images of candidates from the previous three US Congressional elections. Students were asked to determine who appeared more competent as each applicant appeared on the computer screen. On average, the students correctly predicted the election winner over 70% of the time.

Surprisingly Accurate

Evidence suggests that some of our rapid assessments about other individuals are correct. It is simple to determine if someone is extroverted or shy. Several studies have found that judging someone's extroversion by glancing at their photos (even for 50 milliseconds) predicts how extroverted they are. But we're also fast to make correct judgments about factors that appear to be far more challenging to anticipate, such as how much money a CEO will make for the firm in a given year or someone's love interest to us. For example, personality attributes inferred from executive faces predict their leadership skills, as assessed by bottom-line earnings. The impacts are just as significant whether the photo is current or from the leader's undergraduate days.

According to research, 5-minute video clips and even photographs of women's faces may effectively predict their sexual beliefs and activities. Similarly, seeing a flash of a glance for 40 milliseconds — 10 times faster than a typical eye-blink is needed to determine whether a male was homosexual or a woman was a lesbian, and thinking about it longer made their "gaydar" less accurate. They choked when asked to think carefully about their decision (rather than just acting on instinct), producing no better results than random guessing.

The Importance of Being Aware

Other than providing for exciting water cooler discussion, why do scientists care enough to spend their time and everyone's money (public funds supported the majority of these studies) researching topics like "gaydar"? The science of snap judgments entails far more than merely discovering a few intriguing facts about what we can tell by glancing at each other. Knowing how we chop individuals up daily helps us understand how the mind and brain operate and what this may signify for society.

Most of the time, we do this automatically or intuitively, behind the thoughts we hear ourselves having in our brains. Sometimes our instincts about another individual are correct: "She appears pleasant. I'll get directions from her." But, at times, such sensations may be tainted by unjustified assumptions, prejudices, and stereotypes that taint our actions, conversations, and decisions: "He appears honest. I'll invest with him." Perhaps our parents taught us not to judge a book by its cover. Even though the cover doesn't always communicate the whole story, its title could. We are studying the science of snap judgments teaches us which emotions to pay attention to and which to disregard.

Understanding how our minds put information about other people together exposes us to how others perceive us at first glance and helps us avoid making poor decisions when evaluating other people. We like to communicate with individuals we understand and with whom we have enough in common to have a discussion. The prospect of fresh ideas, new looks, and new people can be thrilling — but they must not be so unlike that we feel threatened by them. And we don't recognize how much this need for similarity influences our decisions.

Assume you're interviewing someone for a position in your lab. After eliminating applicants who lack the necessary abilities or experience, you are left with a small group of equally qualified candidates. When making a final decision, you strive to ask creative questions to each applicant and try to read between the lines in letters of reference and compare data. Then you learn that the candidate across the desk from you like zombie movies. You now regard her as more than just a highly qualified candidate; you see her as someone with whom you can discuss, reminisce, or maybe see a movie after work. She has a slight edge over the other applicants since she can provide you with something you aren't aware of.

Interpersonal relationships aren't usually that clear. Sometimes we go with our gut instinct that one individual will be easier to get along with than another.

Our unconscious mind is so good at sizing up others that even the most innocuous cues may trigger sensations that color and drive our thinking — and can have significant social consequences.

According to research dating back nearly 50 years, teachers see beautiful youngsters as intelligent. This persuades instructors to pay more attention to those students, attaining extraordinary academic achievement. And this tends to support the first rash assessment of the child's IQ.

When to Trust Your Gut

Knowing when to question our ideas can help us spot mistakes, but it can also help us understand when to listen to what our unconscious brains are saying to us. Let's say the cute guy next door welcomes you with a grin and tells you how delighted he is to see you, but something doesn't feel right. A quick look at his smile might help determine his sincerity: Is he simply smiling with his mouth, or is he also smiling with his eyes? When someone is genuinely joyful, the corners of their eyes crinkle instinctively – a muscular action that is difficult to imitate. Without those wrinkles, his smile could be more courteous than eager. You don't have to be a nonverbal behavior specialist to make effective decisions:

Your instincts are already telling you what to do. It's only a sense, like any other, and it's up to us to know when to listen ("Ouch! Take my hand off that scorching burner") and when to disregard ("Ouch! The flu vaccination needle hurts, but I shouldn't move my arm until it's finished").

Looking into the cogs and wheels of our intuition about others might help us make wise judgments. Do I choose a longer queue at the supermarket since the cashier in the shorter line is friendly?

Knowing oneself is the beginning point for many things, and understanding the workings of our thoughts may help us make decisions that are beneficial for ourselves and the collective community.

Even our forewarning moms can't help but judge books by their covers, whether we believe it's right or not. So, when we go through life's library, gazing at all the faces on the shelves and in the stacks, we must be conscious of where our thinking habits may lead us: correctness or error.

❑

CHAPTER 5

Risk-taking and Decision-making

Entrepreneurial risk-taking is essential in many disciplines, including innovation and entrepreneurship. Even though the results of taking calculated risks might occasionally be disastrous, humanity must continue to take calculated chances if it is to evolve. In its most basic form, risk-taking may be described as acts performed while the consequences or probabilities of events are unknown or just partially understood. An examination of the comprehensive literature shows frequent references to individuals' risk-taking disposition. Risk-taking and other versions of the construct, such as global risk-taking, risk orientation at work, risk attitude, and domain-specific risk-taking, are currently measured using multiple validated instruments.

Several studies have found that risk-taking is an essential predictor of creativity in various disciplines, including business and demanding sports like rock climbing. The following is a basic explanation of the function of risk-taking in entrepreneurship, which is directly related to innovation and decision-making.

Most businesses' performance is determined by their executives' ability to assess risks and choose which course to take. Risk and ambiguity are two components of uncertainty, and decision-makers' ability to tolerate ambiguity and risk influences their choices. Successful high-risk decision-makers regularly find more chances in dangerous circumstances, and their preference for higher risk presents itself in more confidence in their decision. Sim Sitkin and Amy Pablo established three categories of elements that impact a decision-choice maker's the more or less hazardous approach to a problem: features of the individual decision-maker, characteristics of the organizational setting, and parts of the problem itself.

They specifically address nine critical predictors of risk behavior: three individual characteristics: risk preferences, risk perceptions, and risk propensity; four organizational factors that have a direct impact on individual behavior: group composition, cultural risk values, leader risk orientation, and administrative control systems; and two problem-related characteristics: problem familiarity and problem framing. Decision-makers are heavily pushed to take measured risks, as erroneous judgments can send a firm or the entire economy crashing down, as was the case with highly leveraged risk-taking decisions made by bankrupted corporations such as Lehman Brothers and AIG. It is critical to understand the many elements that influence this construct. Let us begin with the fundamental dispute over whether risk-taking is a circumstance or a characteristic, followed by a quick discussion of internal elements such as intrinsic motivation and demography, as well as external influences such as culture, group dynamics.

Because every coin has two sides, it is critical to grasp the other side of risk-taking. Without question, taking risks offers advantages, but some aspects to consider before venturing into the unknown. First and foremost, the choice should be founded on factual facts; prior knowledge or expertise, if any, may be precious in acquiring further information. Time should be spent planning for the worst-case situation based on this knowledge. Other criteria include, but are not limited to, the risk-to-benefit ratio; the scale of the impact; whether a person will feel the risk's effects/consequences, group, organization, or the general public; long-term and short-term effects; and so on. When a risk taker considers all of these aspects, essentially accepting the possible hazards of failure, this is a calculated risk, instead of a total lack of awareness of these factors—taking risks on faith.

Risk-takers may become victims of what is known as a "halo effect," which occurs when one trait or just one aspect dominates all other variables or when the individual unknowingly overlooks other factors and focuses on only one. For example, the large expanse of the Quebec forest enticed International Telephone and Telegraph (ITT) management to decide to establish a multi-million dollar chemical cellulose mill there without thoroughly assessing considerations such as political and labor hazards in French-speaking Quebec. The lack of rigorous analysis resulted in a $600 million loss on the project.

Furthermore, it has been discovered that.

1. past success leads to a willingness to take risks,
2. individuals focus on highly favorable outcomes even if they are less likely to occur, and
3. Risk-taking propensity is negatively associated with the time required to reach a decision and the amount of information based on the decision.

Ronald Taylor and Marvin Dunnette discovered that high-risk-takers make faster judgments based on less information in terms of risk-taking proclivity. However, they digest each piece of information slowly.

Risk-taking: Is it a situational attribute or a trait? Potential Antecedents

Scholars have questioned whether risk-taking is a situational or dispositional trait. Some people firmly believe that the situation determines a person's risk-taking behavior. Prospect Theory, developed by Daniel Kahneman and Amos Tversky, proposes that framing a problem influences individual risk behavior. Another critical factor in determining how much danger people are willing to accept is their opinion of their talents in the circumstance. The more capacity, the larger the danger that the individual can endure.

On the other hand, other experts have long recognized that logical calculations and individual risk preferences influence dangerous judgments. As a result, a growing body of data demonstrates that risk-taking is genetic rather than situational. This viewpoint is congruent with Big Five personality theory, which argues that risk proclivity is a subset of extraversion.

Although it is a characteristic, research is still inconclusive, and whether risk-taking is a multidimensional construct remains unanswered. Other attributes and emotions have been shown to have a positive (raise) or negative (reduce) influence on a person's risk-taking behavior. Individual variations in trait anxiety, concern, and social anxiety were also linked to risk avoidance. There is growing popularity in understanding the function of sensation seeking and certain emotions in risk-taking.

Emotions and Sensation Seeking

Researchers discovered higher sensation seeking as a personality trait distinguishing risk-takers from non-risk-takers. Sensation seeking is described as a need for new and different experiences and a readiness to accept risks for the sake of those experiences.

Emotions also influence risk-taking behavior. They function as relevant types of information, signaling the presence of specific hazards to avoid or advantages to get. Affective states are transient moods or emotional experiences, whereas affective characteristics are tendencies to have such experiences (positive and negative affect). On the other hand, positive and negative effects boost and diminish risk-taking proclivity. An intriguing study discovered that fear and anger negatively impacted risk perception. Jennifer Lerner and Dacher Keltner found that although afraid individuals are pessimistic and make risk-averse decisions, angry people make optimistic risk-seeking choices.

The Influence of Intrinsic Motivation, Achievement Need, and Self-Efficacy

Individuals are said to be intrinsically driven when they do a task because the work itself fascinates them rather than the activity's results. Intrinsic motivation is a critical component of creativity connected to higher risk-taking, linked to innovation.

Risk-taking and the urge for accomplishment are inextricably linked. High need achievers favor moderate degrees of risk, whereas low need achievers choose extremely low or high levels of risk. The following is a synopsis of research relating the two constructs: Individuals with a strong desire for accomplishment establish demanding objectives of moderate complexity, attain their goals via work and talent, accept personal responsibility for decisions, and take modest risks.

Self-efficacy is an individual's conviction in their capacity to complete the work at hand and accomplish the intended outcome. People who have a strong sense of self-efficacy are less likely to be afraid of failure and are more inclined to take measured chances than irresponsible ones. They are more prone to establish challenging objectives, put up the effort, and persevere in the face of adversity.

Other elements that influence risk-taking

An individual's risk-taking behavior is impacted by gender, age, group, and culture.

Gender and age differences in risk-taking

Historically, women were characterized as cautious and risk-averse, in contrast to men, who were thought to have a higher risk proclivity. One of the causes was that women were pressured to conform to be more conservative than men. However, in the late 1980s, the societal viewpoint shifted, with a significant increase in female workers and a significant growth in female entrepreneurs. As a result, gender inequalities in risk-taking behavior are thought to have been minimized.

The association between risk-taking and age has gotten a lot less attention, especially among senior individuals. Michael Wallach and Nathan Kogan examined risk-taking behavior in college-age and older men and women. They discovered that males and females in the older sample were comparatively risk-averse than their younger counterparts. One explanation might be the significant rise in obligations as individuals advance in age; they come across marriage, children, and financial difficulties. These duties discourage people from taking risks that they might have handled earlier in their growth. Compared to younger persons, older ones have reduced accomplishment motivation.

In particular, according to early research conducted by Heinz Heckhausen, a considerable reduction in many people's level of accomplishment motivation tends to emerge until around or beyond the age of 50. As previously demonstrated, risk-taking is intimately related to the demand for achievement, which exhibits a continuous reduction with age. However, stereotyping should be avoided because older people take significant risks, such as Walt Disney, who mortgaged his home to complete Disneyland.

Groups Taking Risks

The vast majority of research supports understanding the risky shift phenomenon—on average, individuals would privately propose a higher level of risk-taking following group discussion than before. According to Roger Brown, group discussions lead to members changing their individual decisions toward the appropriate social-cultural value. This shift is explained by the self-image maintenance mechanism, which states that people believe their actions are more congruent with commonly held ideals than comparable others' decisions. When they realize that other people's actions are more compatible with these ideals than their own, they attempt to protect their self-image by shifting their choices to the extremes.

Taking Risks Across Cultures

Risk-taking is a relatively stable personality trait learned at a young age. According to research, cultural variations have been a factor in the diverse risk evaluations made by different people and groups. For example, Melissa Finucane discovered in 2000 that whites were less anxious about a set of nominated dangers across various American groups than non-whites, with white males being the least hesitant and non-white women being the most concerned. This gap might be related to white men's socioeconomic advantage, making them less risk-averse than non-whites.

According to another study, Chinese individuals are less risk-averse than Americans. This could not be ascribed to China and the United States of America being incredibly different on the individualistic-collectivist continuum. China is a strongly collectivistic society, and the United States of America is highly individualistic. Collectivism denotes a culture in which social solid and individual relationships, with people belonging to strong, cohesive groupings, whereas individualism denotes fewer links between individuals, emphasizing freedom. "Collectivism functions as implicit collective insurance against catastrophic losses," Elke Weber, Christopher Hsee, and Joanna Sokolowska noted (1998, p. 174). Furthermore, they pointed out that, while people from collectivistic cultures may be less risk-averse to material or financial risks, this will not be the case for social risks, as social networks are critical in such cultures.

Another research, led by Larry Cummings, Donald Harnett, and Owen Stevens, evaluated risk-taking behavior in five geographic clusters with reported scores ranging from 16 to 48. (with lower scores indicating risk-taking and higher scores depicting risk aversion). Americans had the highest risk-taking proclivity (31.9), followed by Spain (33.4), Greece (35.6), Scandinavia (35.7), and Central Europe (35.8). Aside from cultural variations, risk-taking may be influenced by situational variables such as the nations' current economic, social, and political environments.

In the subject of risk-taking, further study is needed. Traditionally, researchers have concentrated on the psychological and demographic features distinguishing risk-takers from controls; nevertheless, substantial variation may occur within risk-taking populations. Furthermore, it is crucial to highlight that people are not solely classed as risk-takers or non-risk-takers, but maybe selective risk-takers, depending on the importance of the goals or some other element influencing their choice.

Entrepreneurial training

Understandingwhatmotivatesentrepreneurship is still one of the most significant problems in management study. Is it, for example, exposure to a business education that drives the desire to start a firm? What variables influence entrepreneurial education? Following in the footsteps of Zhao et al. (2005), we investigated the extent to which students perceived they had learned about four critical skills required by entrepreneurs: (1) recognizing opportunities for new business, (2) evaluating opportunities, (3) starting a business, and (4) organizational entrepreneurship. The panel will give specific facts and analyze disparities in entrepreneurship education among Chinese, Filipino, and American college students. The emphasis will be on instructional style and other new teaching methods such as service-learning, which substantially aids pedagogy and improves student learning, particularly in the field of entrepreneurship.

Cultural Values' Influence on Entrepreneurial Intention

Entrepreneurial intent (EI) is the desire to start a business. According to Krueger and Carsrud (1993), Entrepreneurial intent is the "single best predictor" of later entrepreneurial action. In other words, cognition both precedes and predicts future conduct. Furthermore, while a "great business concept" may be the spark that ignites the choice to start a new enterprise, data suggests that most entrepreneurs decide to start a business before deciding on the sort of firm (Brockhaus, 1987).

Entrepreneurs in general, high growth, and lifestyle

The entrepreneurial aim is most likely not a single concept. While it is feasible to tap into "universal entrepreneurial purpose," various variants should also be examined. The general entrepreneurial purpose is to create one's firm or become self-employed, motivated by both a desire for autonomy and a goal for financial gain. The second sort of entrepreneurship has been labeled "high growth." It refers to the purpose of acquiring or starting a firm to rapidly grow it, maybe into a worldwide enterprise, an industry leader, or a public corporation through an initial public offering (Siebert & Hills, 2005; Hmieleski & Corbett, 2006).

We define the third sort of entrepreneurial intent as lifestyle EI, or the desire to create a firm to gain autonomy and a specific level of living quality. We took the word from John Isaacson (2007), a member of an angel investor organization, who stated that investors prefer to avoid entrepreneurs who desire autonomy and a particular lifestyle - doing what they want to do – without the requirement for a significant return on investment or a strategy for quick expansion. Our idea of the lifestyle entrepreneur may be akin to what Bird (1998) described as a "craftsman entrepreneur," or persons who start new businesses to employ their abilities autonomously. McGuire (2009) discovered three robust components and accurate scales for each type of EI assessment.

Culture and Extrinsic Factors' Influence on Entrepreneurial Education

Culture is a set of socially created meanings, values, and ideas that have emerged from a group's effective coping with environmental issues and the complications of organizing social connectionsandintegratingindividuals. Common values distinguish one community from another aside from symbols, stories, rituals, heroes, and artifacts (Morris et al., 2002). Because groups create and pass on values to new members, it is frequently feasible to describe a group (for example, a society) based on the cultural values that its members share. Each person has a unique collection of cultural values. While aggregates (correctly computed) of individuals belonging to the same group (say, a nation) represent valid generalizations, individual variances exist and can be considerable - even within the most cohesive group.

Even though several studies have been undertaken, Morris et al. noted a "notable paucity of focus [...of research] given to the role of values in successful entrepreneurial undertakings." 2002, p. 35 Cultural values have been demonstrated to influence numerous social entrepreneurial outcomes, including economic creativity and innovation (Shane,1992, 1993, 1995; Guerrero & McGuire, 2001; Williams &

McGuire, 2005). Ethnicity and race, sometimes connected with cultural values, have also been linked to entrepreneurial activity. Ramachadran and Shah (1999), for example, discovered considerable disparities in the size and success rate of new enterprises founded by members of different ethnic groups in Africa.

According to one survey, African Americans establish new enterprises at three times the rate of white Americans in the United States (Kollinger & Minniti, 2006). Minniti and Bygrave (2003) discovered considerable disparities in entrepreneurship rates among ethnic groups within the same society, i.e., with identical economic and institutional features. Davidsson and Wilkund (1997) found substantial differences between entrepreneurs and non-entrepreneurs, implying that such disparities in values will be connected with entrepreneurial intent.

We measure culture on six dimensions using a validated research instrument:

1. Doing vs. being orientation,

2. Determinism vs. free will,

3. Power distance, and
4. Uncertainty. Uncertainty vs. Acceptance Avoidance,
5. Individualism vs. Collectivism, and
6. Facework all topics to consider.

Learning From My Experiences

Being an entrepreneur isn't really about starting a business. It's a way of looking at the world: seeing opportunities where others see obstacles, taking risks when others take refuge.

— Michael Bloomberg

Let me take you to the year 1986 of my life. The year was full of fantastic opportunities as I gained confidence as a Garment Exporter. But I had a big vision to fulfill, and destiny had beautiful plans for me. I decided to explore opportunities outside of India. This might sound quite weird to my readers since they know that neither I am a man with handsome money as working capital to invest nor had a Godfather in the business industry for hand-holding. Whatever learnings I have, are the sheer outcome of my mistakes or achievements.

I read about 'the law of attraction' in many books such as The Secret but never thought it could work so perfectly in my life. My desire to expand my business was so strong that the universe made it possible for me. One of my friends extended the help of arranging my tickets for New York, which made my prospects stronger. Another friend of mine agreed to lend me 300 dollars to meet our initial expenses of my visit, and the rest could be taken care of by my childhood friend in New York.

I had not much to spend, so my focus was to get orders for my business. I got a couple of orders from New York, but the major challenge was arranging the working capital. Again I took a quick and risky decision to take a credit of 2000 dollars from my friend, keeping my ego aside. Even my customer agreed to give me an advance of 2000 dollars to complete his order. It might sound unbelievable to you, but our intent is good and hard work speaks for our credibility.

With a working capital of 4000 dollars in hand, I was determined to expand overseas. Time favored me, and I completed my orders well on time. On my second visit to New York, I was introduced to a renowned buyer who guided and trained me for having big orders. He asked to take up his order of 50,000 to 100,000 units. I had never thought that such a moment would ever come in my life when I would be showered with loads of blessings by the Almighty. But my limitation was that I couldn't meet the requirements of such big orders. Instead of lingering on my aspirations of becoming rich overnight, I decided to be crystal clear with my client. I told him frankly that fulfilling big orders was beyond my capacity. I owned a small factory which can produce only 5000 units in a month.

My client was very impressed with my honesty and integrity, so he agreed to give me a small order.

On his visit to India, one fine Sunday morning, he called me up and expressed his wish to see my factory. I picked him up on my bike from Surya Hotel New Friends Colony, where he was staying, and took him to my factory. He gave me two to three hundred samples to work on and assured me to provide more work in the coming. He was going to South India to meet some more exporters, so I decided to complete the work within a week to show him on his way back. Again, staying for long hours in the factory proved fruitful, and the order was finished in a week. He was impressed with me rather than surprised as other exporters needed one month to complete the same assignment.

He again offered a 50000 units order along with a letter of credit and raw material to finish the order. Now there was no looking back. Year after year, my turnover increased with leaps and bounds. The first year was eight lacs; the second year was closed with 80 lacs of turnover, and the third year we went up to 8 Cr.

When you work hard, opportunities glide your way. Successful people recognize them and turn those opportunities in their favor. Our dependency was only on two or three international clients in the US. We wanted to explore more countries. So, the European market was identified as the target market. I took the address book of the directory of buyers in Germany and landed up in Frankfurt, Germany. This time no friend or client assistance stepped along with me on the foreign land, but my experience accompanied me on every client visit. After a few rejections, I started calling buyers; one Indian buyer wished to meet me. He showed keen interest in my samples and gave many orders. Now we were catering the market in Germany and those days were the golden ones as now we were in two countries.

The next step was to get ourselves registered for getting recognition on government platforms. So, in 1995 I decided to get listed on the Bombay Stock Exchange. Soon we realized that we have much more to achieve in the global market as an export business of 30 Cr. export could not compete with the companies like Reliance, Century Mill, Tata Steels. We took assistance from consultants and advisers and got listed, and IPO got over subscribed 300 times. This was another life-changing moment that we experienced as a blessing from Him. We were interviewed on Doordarshan by Jai Ram Ramesh on his famous Business Breakfast show, which broadcasts at the 8 am prime hour.

We go through each day, whether it's excellent or terrible, with the trust that we can conquer any hurdle that comes our way, even though it's not always an easy route to go.

So, when life is pleasant, please make the most of it by thoroughly appreciating and receiving it. Remember that life does not endure forever and that better days are on the way when things aren't going so well. We should maintain contact with family and friends and make no room for despair or loneliness.

❑

CHAPTER 6

You Cannot Have Control of Everything

Reinhold Niebuhr, an American theologian, penned a prayer poem in the years leading up to World War II that became far more famous than he could have imagined. It begins with praying to God for "grace to accept with peace the things that cannot be changed, bravery to change the things that should be changed, and discernment to differentiate the one from the other."

This tidbit has been taken to heart by many self-help seekers, but it may also be viewed as excellent business counsel. There will always be things that a single CEO will be unable to change. Macroeconomic forces, for example, are outside the boundaries of what a business can directly influence. As editor-at-large Leigh Buchanan points out, the quantity and quality of a company's potential employment pool are determined by national immigration and education regulations.

We spent time looking for its many implications because this topic is about putting together the best team possible. The State of Hiring 2018 package, which was launched by Buchanan's essay, highlights the innovative and inventive methods in which organizations find employees in a tight labor market, ranging from going beyond the traditional workforce to accessing talent from all over the world.

Of course, once you've hired all of your dream staff, the next step is to keep them all.

Leadership is the key to changing what needs to be changed. If you put together and keep an excellent team, you'll discover that the breadth of what can't be altered is considerably narrower than you expected.

Some individuals hesitate to recognize a harsh reality in life: you do not influence many events.

Some people who oppose the truth become control freaks. They micromanage, refuse to delegate duties, and attempt to compel others to change. They believe that if they can obtain enough control over other people and the conditions in which they find themselves, they will prevent unpleasant things from happening.

Others are aware that they cannot prevent awful things from happening, yet they are concerned. They are worried about various issues, ranging from natural calamities to lethal illnesses. Their anxieties keep them busy, but they eventually waste their time and energy since worrying is ineffective.

Here are six suggestions to help you if you spend much time worrying about matters over which you have little control:

1. Figure out what you have control over

When you find yourself worrying, take a moment to consider the areas over which you have control. A storm cannot be avoided, but it may be prepared for. You cannot control people's reactions, but you do control how you respond to them.

Recognize that there are times when you have no control over anything but your effort and attitude. You'll be far more effective if you concentrate your attention on the things you can control.

2. Concentrate on your power

You can impact people and events, but you can't make them happen. So, while you can provide your child with the tools he needs to succeed in school, you can't force him to get a 4.0 GPA. And, while you may arrange a great party, you can't make people have a good time.

Focus on modifying your behavior to have the maximum impact. Set appropriate boundaries for yourself and be a good role model.

When you are concerned about someone else's decisions, express your worries, but just once. Don't try to change those who don't want to change.

3. Recognize your fears

Consider what you are worried will happen. Do you foresee a disastrous outcome? Do you have doubts about your abilities to deal with disappointment?

In most cases, the worst-case scenario isn't as dreadful as you may think. There's a decent possibility you're more powerful than you realize.

However, people are sometimes so obsessed with the concept, "I can't let my business fail," that they neglect to ask themselves, "What would I do if my business failed?" Recognizing that you can manage the worst-case scenario will focus on more productive activities.

4. Recognize the difference between ruminating and problem-solving.

It's not beneficial to replay discussions in your thoughts or imagine disastrous situations repeatedly. However, resolving an issue is.

So consider if your thinking is productive. Keep working on solutions if you are actively tackling a problem, such as identifying strategies to improve your chances of success.

Change the channel in your thoughts if you're wasting time ruminating. Recognize that your thoughts are unproductive, and get up and do something for a few minutes to refocus your mind on something more useful.

5. Make a stress-management strategy

Exercising, eating healthy, and getting plenty of sleep are just a few of the things you should do to look for yourself. It would be best to spare time to control your stress to work more productively.

Find healthy stress relievers such as meditation, socializing with friends, or participating in hobbies.

Take note of your stress level and how you handle hardship.

Eliminate harmful coping mechanisms, such as excessive drinking or whining to others.

6. Create positive affirmations

I have two mantras that I repeat to myself to remind me to act or relax. "Make it happen," the first says. "Make it happen," I urge myself anytime I catch myself saying things like, "I hope I do okay today." It seems to remind me that I have control over my actions.

Then, if I find myself worried about something I have no control over, such as "I wish it doesn't rain on Saturday," I tell myself, "I can manage it." Having those quick little phrases on hand keeps me from wasting time on things I have no control over. I'll either do everything I can to make it happen or live with the things I can't change.

Create a few healthy mantras to keep you psychologically strong. Those quotes will help you overcome self-doubt, terrible prophecies, and continuous ruminating.

Learning from My Mistakes

When things don't go our way, getting caught up in negative thinking is all too easy.

We float into places and thoughts over which we have no control.

We begin to ruminate on all things that aren't going our way, thinking about the horrible things that may happen next.

We lose sight of our part in molding our world, and our judgment becomes clouded.

Today, this may be the case.

We're fighting a worldwide epidemic, and I can guarantee you that each one of us has good and terrible days.

On good days, we endeavor to be upbeat and productive. We wallow in fear of forecasting what the future will be like on terrible days. We picture it, then begin to experience it, leaving us feeling helpless and terrified.

But there is a workaround.

Whenever I notice myself shifting from a good to a negative perspective, I do my best to focus on the essential part of all.

I ask myself three questions: What worries me?

What am I able to control?

What is important to me, and what can I do about it?

When we concentrate on what we can manage, our ideas strengthen us, and, as a result, we experience happy feelings.

In March 2020, the world was infected with COVID-19. For decades, India's services economy has fueled the development and reduced unemployment in the world's second-most populated country. The coronavirus epidemic prompted calls for an urgent economic to rebalance toward manufacturing.

High-contact service employment, ranging from airlines to hotels and shopping malls to multiplexes, was the first to go under during the virus's lengthy lockdown. The sector's fall, which generally contributes to 55 percent of the GDP, drives people to look for jobs on remote firms or in the smaller manufacturing industry.

Many enterprises had come to a halt, and owners were looking for optimism in trainers and mentors. My one-on-one coaching and business networking events moved online, and I began mentoring company owners via Zoom sessions. *I realized the positive aspect of being close to technology as it has saved my hours in commuting and fatigue, which I used to feel after the journeys. My productivity increased, and I could spare my time writing books and thinking of new and innovative ways to expand my business. I wrote a book, 'Closing Your Sales' and complemented it with my Turbo Sales Blueprint Program. It was a "365 Days Sales, Marketing, and Business Growth Strategies Program" on YouTube. I expanded and invested in online platforms and started conducting webinars. I created a community of credible business owners for the "Complete Business and Life Mastery Program (CBLM)," which became highly successful.*

When the world was suffering from setbacks, my perseverance and desire to help business owners presented an ideal opportunity to expand my Tajurba Business Networking Community to the rest of India. Chapters were being established in Mumbai, Dubai, Kolkata, and the south of India.

It's a lovely feeling to have business owners with years of experience joining you to learn from your expertise.

❑

CHAPTER 7

Quick Goals and Quick Decision-making

Making decisions, both primary and little, is crucial to a company's success. There is a need to solve a problem or capitalize on an upcoming opportunity; therefore, decisions are made. Making educated judgments requires gathering the appropriate amount of information and feedback from relevant stakeholders.

Identifying a goal, gathering relevant and essential information, and analyzing options are all part of the decision-making process. Although the notion appears straightforward, many people neglect some crucial phases and hazards when making decisions. It is critical to make the best judgments feasible under the conditions whenever possible.

Making thoughtful judgments has at least four significant advantages:

1. Good judgments have a longer shelf life. A well-thought-out choice will seldom need to be revisited, and it may occasionally endure the whole existence of an organization.

2. Sound judgments consider both internal and external influences. A decision-maker should look at a corporation as a whole. Internal and external variables can influence the selection and the company's strategy.

3. Sound judgment eliminates conflicts of interest. During the decision-making process, transparency and stakeholder buy-in reduce the likelihood of queries or objections after the fact. The advantages of this procedure include keeping the company on track and focused and reducing churn.

4. Good judgments work better in the long run. Good decisions get the decision-maker, department, and firm closer to their objectives and solve the initial problem.

What Is the First Step in a Decision-Making Process?

The most critical initial stage in any process is explicitly articulating the necessity for a decision. Although it may appear prominent, many firms focused on moving may neglect this stage. Outline this target decision in as much detail as feasible. Include why this choice is crucial to your company's or your department's goals. It would be best to justify why you first chose the aim demanding a decision.

It is impossible to choose or achieve a goal in a vacuum. Unless it is aligned with a business requirement, it is a waste of time and money. As a result, the first stage in any decision-making process is to confirm that your decision is genuinely necessary in the first place and that it represents a broader organizational aim.

How to Boost Decision-Making Capacity

It is vital to incorporate evaluation into the process. Ensure that at least one of the phases involves evaluating and reviewing the process and its outcomes, particularly for future use. Additionally, obtain advance approval from all stakeholders (including those involved in the process) and keep them informed. Capture metrics throughout the journey that demonstrate achievements, failures, the comparative benefits of choices you've examined, and competition research to support your replies and keep the process running smoothly.

Traditional Business Decision-Making Processes

Before delving into the many phased plans in decision-making, let's look at some specific sorts of decision-making. Various alternative accurate decision-making methods may be employed that comprise several phases. The most common and widely used procedures consist of five, six, seven, or eight stages.

Of course, the number of stages will vary if you divide activities completed in a single step into multiple phases. Whatever procedure you use, the last stage is assessment, and wise businesses will take the time to do so. Organizations that use this review phase over time can obtain substantial savings in time and attention. It also contributes to the general health and strength of the firm by ensuring institutional learning.

Decision-Making Process in Eight Steps

The eight-step method includes data collection and the identification of essential criteria. A comprehensive brainstorming session is usually held to cast a wide net when exploring ideas. The following are the eight steps:

Determine the final objective and the need for the decision.

Collect all pertinent information.

Determine your criteria for evaluating all of the choices.

To assess each possibility, hold a particular brainstorming session.

Compare all of the options and list their benefits and drawbacks.

Make your choice.

Put the choice into action.

After the fact, evaluate the decision.

What Is the Process of Ethical Decision-Making?

The ethical decision-making process requires that all decisions include evaluating and selecting options compatible with moral issues. This entails making the most ethical choices possible, regardless of the impact on the bottom line. Ethical decision-making also entails rejecting any possibilities incompatible with ethical standards from the start.

As per the University of California, San Diego, citing the Josephson Institute of Ethics, the three Cs of ethical decision-making are:

Commitment: Never waver from doing or doing the right thing, regardless of the cost.

Consciousness: Instill enough awareness in your team and project members so that they are capable of acting ethically every day with moral conviction.

Competency: The continuing process of analyzing information as you go and weighing possibilities that allow you to make ethical judgments consistently. As the world's conditions change, having a high capacity to analyze these changes is vital to remaining ethical.

Potential Drawbacks of Using a Formal Decision-Making Process

Before going on a decision-making process, it's a good idea to consider some potential dangers. Following a strategy is crucial, but don't follow it "out the window." Here are five potential concerns that might develop when employing a formal decision-making process:

From now on, with Inadequate Information or Relying on a Single Source: If you're going to follow a formal procedure, you'll need data. Document each step and gain approval from your coworkers. Information is power, and acquiring information from relevant yet various sources is essential for strategic thinking.

Too Much Information: Gathering too much or irrelevant information can be overwhelming and confusing, leading decision-makers astray from the issue that requires a choice and how best to get at it.

Putting Too Much Trust in an Option That May Produce Negative Results: As you narrow down on a process and choice, try to discover a viable option or possibilities. Gather enough information during the process to play out scenarios for each selection.

Attempting to Solve the Wrong Problem: If you don't know what's causing the problem, doing research first might be crucial. For example, if your manufacturing output has been declining, don't assume that you need additional workers, or more factory hours, or anything else until you've identified the underlying cause of the slowdown.

Being too rigid or attached to the process: It is possible to adhere to a decision-making process so rigidly that a firm's organic character, employees, and needs are sidelined or disregarded. Even if you are following a business decision-making process methodically and confidently, you and your team must be able to pivot if necessary.

Successes in Decision-Making Processes

In some ways, a company's history mirrors how decisions are made. Some of the world's most successful firms have converted failure into success by concentrating on the final critical phase in all decision-making processes: reviewing the choice after the fact.

Coca-Cola in 1985 is one example of this. According to business and leadership expert John Addison, the firm chose to address the shifting soda industry by producing "new Coke." Unfortunately, the rebranding flopped poorly after three months, forcing the firm to reinstate the old Coca-Cola. The major takeaway: Reversing a course isn't a sign of failure;

instead, it demonstrates a leader's dedication to retaining the company's health as a top priority. Furthermore, it reflects the significance of revisiting and evaluating decisions.

Companies frequently utilize data to test a pilot or program, and if it fails, they may reconsider their choice and alter direction. Giant corporations are continually analyzing data to uncover actionable pathways in other circumstances. These three businesses achieved success by making decisions based on data and stakeholder feedback:

According to Harvard Business Review, Google established a people analytics department to assist the corporation in making HR choices based on data, such as determining if managers make a difference in the performance of their teams. To answer this question, the department used performance reviews and employee surveys. The organization discovered that a laser focus on performance did not suggest the best or happiest teams; instead, managers with great people skills had the top-performing groups and employees who were delighted and remained with the company longer.

In the initial years of Amazon, its data analysts observed that customers who purchased a specific book, CD, or DVD were also more likely to buy another product. Perhaps these comparable goods were created by the same author or artist, or maybe the films starred the same actors or dealt with similar themes. Perhaps these were just hot titles that the client desired. Editors were taking on the position of "trusted adviser" at the time, offering suggestions based on purchases via emails and other human-created material. However, the corporation believed an automated tool might supplement the human editors' proposal. Amazon eventually opted to utilize the data to develop its first, primitive personalization tool. The firm saw a significant increase in sales after presenting customers with things that other customers previously purchased.

These are examples of accomplishments that rely on sound decision-making; however, not all decisions are successful. Continuously analyzing and reconsidering choices is a hallmark of a mature organization; otherwise, judgments may result in public failure.

Failures in Decision-Making Processes

Companies' inability to adapt, evolve, or compete successfully is unlikely to be attributed to a single faulty choice or process failure. Nonetheless, companies can doom themselves if they do not adequately acquire data, analyze preferences, and evaluate decisions. Let's enunciate some examples of businesses that did not use or learn from their decision-making processes:

Blockbuster and Borders: Instead of examining data objectively, both of these once-successful brick-and-mortar enterprises exploited statistics to support their prejudices. Instead of responding to the internet's difficulties and potential, their websites and physical locations eventually collapsed.

For decades, Kodak was synonymous with photography in all of its manifestations.

However, it did not look courageously at the changing environment of digital photography. Even after acquiring Ofoto, it failed to capitalize on and commercialize the opportunity. With Kodak Gallery, which Shutterfly later bought, the corporation entered the online picture gallery area late and silently.

Newspapers: It's difficult to imagine a whole business collapsing due to poor decision-making and denial, but that's what happened to newspapers in the late 1990s. While some institutions, such as the New York Times and the Washington Post, have adapted to digital media, most city newspapers are still suffering. Holding on to outdated business models has never helped any company make sound, forward-thinking decisions.

Learning From My Experiences

I have always been inquisitive to learn new things in life. The desire to update myself with the changing scenarios lures me. I heard about Objective Key Results long back in 2017 when

John Doerr published an OKR book, "Measure What Matters: How Google, Bono, and the Gates Foundation Rock the World with OKRs."

I realized that when systems and processes play a vital role in small enterprises, what takes them back to implementing the OKRs in their operations.

This thought gave birth to a revolutionary phase of my life wherein I guided my CBLM Group for OKR. The results are so enthralling that I was amazed to see SMEs sweeping with crores of turnover in the small span of 90 days. Soon success stories became the talk of the town, and the most significant event in the history of OKR for SMEs took unbelievable shape on 2 October 2021. More than 150 entrepreneurs across India celebrated their achievements in the Jashn-E-OKR Event.

This quick decision to be a certified OKR coach has doubled the opportunities life has stored for me.

I often quote this,

"People with top deliberative strength overthink, and the opportunity passes away. Never let it happen in your life. Think wisely, but a delayed decision is not worthy of anything."

❑

CHAPTER 8

Do Not Let Your Emotions Get in The Way of Your Decisions

Consider a period when you were pondering a significant choice at work or a high cost, such as purchasing a home, making a substantial financial investment, or establishing a new business. Such judgments are inherently complicated, and weighing the advantages and drawbacks of each option may be daunting, no matter how much experience we have in making them. Our emotional reactions to these options may effectively direct our attention and energy toward the components of the decision that we believe are the most essential. However, strong emotions might cause us to make rash or even dangerous judgments.

An interesting example may be seen in the 1991 film "Defending Your Life." In one scene, Daniel Miller (Albert Brooks) prepares for a pay discussion with his boss the next day. He enlists his wife's assistance to test the aggressive negotiation tactic he intends to employ. Daniel refuses every wage offer made by his wife, saying that he cannot accept the position for less than $65,000. As Daniel refuses to move from his place, his wife begins to make increasingly appealing propositions to him.

Consider the following scenario: traveling to work and encountering severe traffic. Later that day, you have a critical meeting with a client interested in placing an order for your company's new product. You were the one who started the product's development and saw it through to completion. So there's a lot on the line for you. You're 45 minutes late for work and enraged by the time you get at the workplace. Because your appointment isn't for another hour, you should be able to put aside your rage by then. In reality, my study indicates that we are frequently unable to do so. Emotions aroused by an incident unrelated to a new scenario might impact our thinking.

In one research, Maurice Schweitzer of the Wharton School and I asked a group of volunteers to estimate a person's weight purely based on a photograph of that individual. Participants were compensated based on the accuracy of their estimates. We invited them to view a brief movie clip after giving us their estimations. Some participants saw a clip from a National Geographic program depicting fish in the Great Barrier Reef. Others viewed a clip from the film My Bodyguard in which a young guy is tormented — a clip that we discovered in a pilot test gets people furious because of the violent and unjust treatment the young man receives. All participants estimated given another participant's estimate of the weight of the individual they had just weighed and asked if they wished to update their first estimate.

For those who viewed the "My Bodyguard" clip, the anger they felt while viewing the video clip transferred over to this following, unrelated job. It caused them to doubt and dismiss the other person's assessments instead of relying on their original assumptions. 74% of these individuals did not place any weight on the advice they were given. In comparison, just 32% of those who viewed the impartial National Geographic video ignored the advice. Ignoring the advice cost them money: listening to it would have improved their judgment accuracy and, consequently, higher remuneration.

According to the findings of this study, anger provoked by a previous, unrelated experience that, from an objective standpoint, should not impact our current judgments or decisions might make us unreceptive to what others have to say. Scott Wiltermuth, the University of Southern California, and Larissa Tiedens of Stanford University discovered in related research that anger triggered by something unrelated to the decision at hand affects how we evaluate the ideas of others. Many vocations need us to assess the views of others, including coworkers, clients, employees, friends, and family members.

Wiltermuth and Tiedens conducted one research in which participants first completed a writing assignment before evaluating ideas supplied by others. Half were encouraged to assume they would be assessing high-quality pictures and would most likely make positive assessments. The other half thought that they would negatively judge and evaluate low-quality ideas. Some participants were instructed to write about a period in their lives when they were furious about the writing assignment. Other participants were asked to write about spending the previous day to achieve emotional neutrality.

As a result, although most participants, whether furious or neutral, preferred to assess good rather than terrible ideas, those who were made angry found the task of evaluating others' low-quality ideas significantly more enticing than those in the control condition. Furthermore, angry participants were less engaged in judging the high-quality thoughts of others than those in the control condition. Anger appears to heighten the attraction of criticizing people and their beliefs.

Our emotions can provide meaningful and valuable feedback on a decision, while irrelevant emotions elicited by an entirely unrelated incident might lead us astray. Consider how your emotional reactions may persist when you enter into essential duties or contemplate a hard decision the next time you drink a bitter cup of coffee or have a disagreement with a loved one. Fortunately, we may frequently select when to do each of the several assigned jobs. This should allow us to examine ideas and guidance from others when we think we are most objectively and capable of doing so.

Emotional Control = Making Better Decisions

Now that we know how we make decisions, the next issue is whether we can make better ones when we're agitated by our emotions.

The answer is YES - it is feasible with practice and patience. Here are six pointers to help you get started.

Take a breather and examine the issue.

This little deed can save you much trouble in the future. Allow your brain enough time to assess the current circumstance so that you can make the best decision. Use this strategy when:

You've been posed a difficult question.

You're irritated and may snap at another person.

Your reaction might spell the difference between a loss and again.

You have a feeling you could say something you later regret.

For more significant decisions (such as marriage or a job change), you may want to spend more time analyzing your alternatives. Why not spend the weekend hiking or meditating? This should clarify your thoughts to consider the advantages and disadvantages of each option.

However, in circumstances where you need to respond quickly, stopping for a second is your hidden weapon for giving superior responses — without being nasty.

Don't always go with your gut instinct

One of our most fundamental instincts is intuition, sometimes known as "gut feeling." It assists us with identifying environmental cues so that we might avoid danger and live. However, avoid relying on this human intuition in games of chance (i.e., situations based on a 50/50 likelihood). Gambling and the stock market are two good examples.

So, when should you go with your gut instinct? When there is a requirement for specific skills or knowledge.

For example, suppose you want to work in the charity sector but have prior expertise in finance. You're concerned that you've made the wrong decision. Using advice #1, take a breather before making a final choice. "How do I feel about this job?" ask yourself. Then, develop a list of the advantages and disadvantages of what may happen if you make the transfer. It's free, it provides you some alone time, and you can go back over your notes afterward for more clarity.

Reduce your alternatives

Have you ever wondered why Trader Joe's keeps its grocery offerings so limited? The larger the variety, the more opportunities to make a wrong judgment. This may seem contradictory, but reducing your alternatives will assist you in avoiding selecting something you'll later regret.

Assume you're a recent graduate with a diverse set of skills: you're excellent with people, can write 500-word press pieces, and don't mind pitching an idea to a room of 100 executives. This implies you can take on a variety of tasks. Sending resumes to 10 or 20 firms at once, on the other hand, will give you a headache. If you do not adapt your application to the abilities most relevant to the job, you may be passed over for the position.

Instead, ask the following questions about two or three companies:

Why do you want to work for these corporations?

Are you qualified for the job you're about to start?

What are their perks/compensation packages?

What kind of experience do you want to receive from them?

How long do you plan on staying?

What are your chances of being hired ahead of other candidates?

Narrowing your options can not only save you much worry, but science indicates you'll be pleased with your decision as well!

Inquire of the majority

Humans are notoriously prone to prejudice. Although some of these biases might help us create ideas, they should not judge. Confidence, for example, is an excellent quality to possess. It enables us to see things positively and effectively market our skills. However, we may become overconfident in our abilities over time. Do you know how even the most powerful CEOs and managers frequently make poor decisions?

Asking for a second opinion is one of the most acceptable methods for making the proper decision, mainly if it includes significant risks. For instance, you are astonished that your organization's head does not approve of the crowdfunding video you recently created. He is confident that it does not represent the group's vision.

This irritates you because you worked on the assignment for days. You now have two options: publish it on the video site without his permission or call a team meeting.

Don't rely just on your intuition or experience. This is because our overconfidence frequently causes us to ignore essential nuances that are critical to the end outcome.

Stay away from burnout

Dr. Lynda Shaw, a cognitive neuroscientist, advises making a big decision.

We know the importance of sleep, but many stay up late to accomplish homework, binge-watch shows, or idly surf through social media. A good night's sleep helps our brains analyze information faster and more accurately, one of the most important benefits of getting enough sleep.

Are you agitated, perplexed, or anxious? Get some sleep. You will not only feel rejuvenated after waking up, but your thinking will be clearer to choose a better alternative.

Everyone is frightened of making the incorrect decision. So, how can you ensure that you get it properly 99 percent of the time? Take proper care of yourself. Emotions do not govern us, although they are integral to our being. You will have fewer regrets about your actions after a deeper understanding of your mind and body.

Learning From My Experiences

"Two roads diverged in a yellow wood,
And sorry, I could not travel both."

"I took the one less traveled by,
And that has made all the difference."
– Robert Frost

Being successful as the Manager in a Garment Export factory has never been my goal in life. I wanted to do something worthwhile, but at the same time, I wanted to achieve something which is claimed to be unachievable. So, I took a decision that was entirely against my family's wishes as I decided to come out of my comfort zone. I decided to quit my work and establish my own business. My family knew that neither I had any experience in the industry nor did I have the working capital to start it, but my intent was clear, and my passion was intense.

I was crystal clear about my mission and vision to be rich enough to support my family with a passive and active income in my twenties. I noticed that the Garment Industry was growing by leaps and bounds those days, and my experience as an employee could be icing on the cake for me. So, I borrowed INR 30,000 and commenced my entrepreneurship journey. At first, it was challenging since I could only support minor orders, but that one move had changed my life.

❑

CHAPTER 9

Using Heuristic Techniques to Your Advantage

What exactly are Heuristics?

Heuristics are problem-solving approaches that produce an immediate and practical answer. Heuristics are utilized when a short-term solution is required instead of business choices requiring significant investigation.

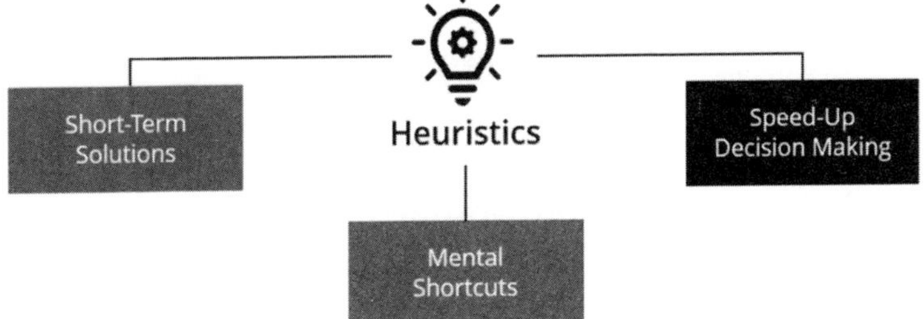

Although heuristics may not produce the most optimum and ideal answer, they do enable businesses to accelerate their decision-making process and get an appropriate solution in the near term.

When flawless answers are unlikely, heuristics can make flawed but acceptable conclusions. Heuristics can also refer to mental shortcuts that aid in decision-making.

- Heuristics are problem-solving approaches that produce an immediate and practical answer.
- When perfect solutions are unlikely, heuristics can make flawed but acceptable conclusions.
- Most heuristic approaches rely on mental shortcuts to judge based on past experiences.

Heuristics are problem-solving approaches that produce an immediate and practical answer.

When perfect solutions are unlikely, heuristics can make flawed but acceptable conclusions.

Most heuristic approaches rely on mental shortcuts to judge based o past experiences.

Heuristics: An Introduction

When confronted with complicated problems with limited time and resources, heuristics can assist businesses in making rapid judgments by utilizing shortcuts and estimated computations. Most heuristic approaches rely on mental shortcuts to judge based on past experiences.

Trial and error, historical data analysis, speculation, and the process of elimination are some of the most prevalent fundamental heuristic procedures. Such strategies often entail using readily available information that is not particular to the problem but is widely applicable. It allows making flawed judgments that will solve the situation satisfactorily in the short run.

Depending on the situation, there may be multiple alternative heuristic techniques available, each of which corresponds to the scope of the problem. Affect, representative, and availability heuristics are examples of heuristics.

Types of Heuristics

Affect Heuristics

Affect heuristics are based on excellent and negative sensations linked with a specific stimulus. It is characterized by fast, reactive feelings based on past ideas. According to the notion of affect heuristics, an individual's emotional response to a stimulus might influence their decisions.

When people have limited time to pause and adequately examine a situation, they may make decisions based on their instant emotional emotions. Rather than undertaking a cost-benefit analysis, affect heuristics are concerned with generating an automatic, reactive response.

Advertisements, for example, have been found to influence customers' emotions and, as a result, their purchase decisions. Advertisements for fast food are one of the most prevalent instances. When fast food companies run promotions, they hope to elicit a positive emotional response that encourages you to think positively about their products.

Individuals who thoroughly consider the hazards and advantages of fast-food consumption may conclude that it is an unhealthy decision. On the other hand, people seldom take the time to assess all they observe and instead make their judgments on an instant, emotional response. Fast food advertisements rely on this form of affect heuristic to elicit a favorable emotional reaction, which leads to sales.

Heuristics for Availability

Availability heuristics are judgments about the possibility of an occurrence made by humans based on information that comes to mind rapidly. People often base their decisions on past knowledge of a circumstance. As a result, we tend to overestimate the chance of an event occurring merely because it occurs swiftly in our minds. These mental shortcuts assist us in making quick judgments, but they can also be erroneous.

Stock prices illustrate the availability heuristic, particularly for freshly public corporations. Many investors engage in new IPOs assuming that the stock price will skyrocket in the following years. Rather than studying the company's fundamentals, investors recall very successful IPOs, such as Amazon or Apple.

Although most initial public offerings (IPOs) underperform, investors tend to overestimate their odds of landing a successful IPO based on past examples that spring to mind. It's a great illustration of availability heuristics.

Heuristics of Representation

We employ representative heuristics to estimate the likelihood of an occurrence based on its resemblance to another event. People tend to overestimate an event's probability of its perceived similarity to another event. When this happens, we overlook the base rate, the actual likelihood of an event occurring regardless of resemblance to past events.

Product packaging is a representative heuristic since buyers prefer to identify exceptional items with their outward package. If a generic brand packages its products to seem like a well-known, high-quality product, people will connect the generic product with the same quality as the branded ones.

Instead of examining the quality of the items, people correlate the quality of the products based on package resemblance.

Learning From My Experiences

Entrepreneurs commonly utilize heuristics to make rapid judgments since uncertainty is a feature of their business. Heuristics are tactics that allow an entrepreneur to create a focused choice based on prior experience instead of being overwhelmed by factual-based argumentation. Heuristics provide an entrepreneur a competitive edge by enabling them to generate fresh insights and successfully manage risk.

I also implemented heuristics in my entrepreneurship journey in 2012. I decided to join a Business Networking platform, BNI. It was an entirely new world of networking for me. But I wanted to explore it to the fullest, so I invested my time and energy in it. I learned to create an influence on the people and other business owners. Soon I started enjoying the power of persuasion.

With my previous life experience, I gathered that nothing comes without hard work and dedicated efforts. I volunteered for the President, then Director, and Support Director in BNI Gurugram. Soon, I became a Super Star of Gurugram on Networking Platforms. I was getting 100/100 scores for passing credible referrals and business. I decided that I would never visit any business meeting without 5 -10 visitors and at least 20-30 referrals with me. I was in BNI for five years and learned all the core skills and integrity of Business Networking.

Now it was time to take a step further, so I decided to open my own Business Networking Platform. It was a risky decision as I could have failed as an influencer or been more successful than the Global Business Networking Platform such as BNI. But I had mentioned earlier that I always preferred to take quick, excellent, and much thought over decisions, so starting my own Business Networking Platform was one of such decisions.

On 17 December 2017, I laid the foundations of the first chapter of Tajurba Business Network in Gurugram with 25 members and 80 visitors. People started joining hands with me, and soon the community was raised to 8 chapters in Delhi NCR. I continuously upgraded myself and stepped into Business Coaching and Mentoring. I did certify coaching from Gallop and Train the Trainer Programs.

Initially, there were a few failures in training as a coach, and I excelled as a Business Coach and Public Speaking Trainer. I gave several Ted talks and trained people for the same. In 2019-2020, my first batch of Public Speaking and Tedx Mastery was held successfully, with almost 100 participants mastering the public speaking skills.

❑

CHAPTER10

Epilogue

Nothing grabs our attention like an unmade decision: Should I take the new job? Which of the following business options is best for me? With limited resources, how can I support my business? If you're having problems making decisions, whether it's due to chronic hesitancy you've always had or a more recent outbreak of decision fatigue, Don't Think and Grow Rich offers a new approach of putting known but frequently forgotten advice into practice: do the next right thing.

What is it that makes us better - or worse - than others at committing to a decision? What are the things preventing us from progressing, and how can we overcome them? Decisions we make have an impact on every part of our life.

But how frequently do we think about our ability to make the best and most innovative decisions? What matters is how we approach and adapt the decision-making process.

Suresh Mansharamani delves into the complexities of decision-making, pushing us to comprehend why we make the decisions we do. He investigates how the actual power of decisions, particularly the most difficult ones, may help us face our anxieties and, as a result, transform how we think about ourselves. Suresh's book is divided into ten parts. He delivers a dynamic and captivating investigation of the decision-making process using brief practical life examples, covering topics such as: What makes us indecisive? What is preventing us from moving forward, and why is it so? Where Art Thou, O Thou? The necessity of taking chances in life and how and where we become stuck. The Decisive Momentum - Maintaining our focus and proactivity. The Deciding Mind is responsible for making the best decisions.

We are led on a trip from the depths of procrastination to the ecstasy of decision-making, using examples from many disciplines. Suresh's unique worldview is informative, thought-provoking, and possibly life-changing, offering a different viewpoint on what to choose at the proverbial fork in the road.

It is possible to clear the decision-making confusion, calm the dread of making the wrong choice, and find the strength to ultimately decide without regret or second-guessing with a simple, meaningful exercise.

Whether you're going through a huge life transition or are wary of the low-grade concern that comes with daily living, the real-life examples in this book will help you make a place for your soul to breathe so you may live life with God at a slower speed and choose your next right thing in life.

❑